Bright Hope

(full colour illustrations)

"I shall love with the colours of a rainbow"

Collected Poems by

Ronald D Lush

First limited edition December 2012.

First Public edition November 2015

Revised edition with minor formatting and spelling changes and new cover. September 2016

ISBN 978-0-9808646-9-4

Poet Author: Ronald D Lush

Collaborative Poem Section contributing Poets:

Ronald D Lush

Inge A Danaher

Lisette Kuiper-Tromp

Art work by Diane Colwell

Chernobyl Photo by Simon Lush

Acknowledgements

I dedicate this book to my family. May it entertain them for years to come.

I wish to thank my family, especially my wife, for their love and appreciation.

My gratitude also goes to:

- My dear friend Inge Danaher for her help in the compilation and publishing of this book and her unwavering and dedicated assistance.
- Dianne Colwell for providing the use of her talents for all the drawings which so wonderfully complement the poems.
- Lisette Kuiper-Tromp and Katey Lomax for their gentle friendship and encouragement.
- The many Poets in Poets of Zarahemla for their continuous positive feedback.
- Angel Radio for their support with broadcasting my poem "I remember Charlie".

Publisher's Foreword

Ronald D Lush is a published UK Poet. Ron's Poems can be funny, romantic or reflective and are always entertaining. Two of his poems have appeared in the local media. Papa's Lullaby was put to music and was successfully used as a fund-raiser by the national paper "The Mirror", when Ron's daughter, at the age of five, lost both her legs to meningitis.

In his poem "I remember Charlie" Ron drew on experiences across several wars including those of his father, grandfather and his own time with the British Army. The poem was aired on Angel Radio for several years on Remembrance Day.

Ron is also known internationally via the online community of Second Life. Many people enjoy listening to him read at public meetings. It is here that Ron and I met in 2007 and co-founded the group Poets of Zarahemla.

We hold virtual events and run Poetry Competitions. We often compose poems together, sometimes with input from other poets. Working with Ron is an enjoyable experience and was especially helpful to me during a period of illness which had me housebound for several years. The virtual world brings together people from all parts of the globe, where in reality we are continents apart.
I hope you enjoy this book as much as I have enjoyed helping Ron put it together.
Inge Danaher.

Author's Foreword

(Are you hungry?)

Welcome to an evening's entertainment with this book of poems. Pull up a comfy chair get ready, make yourself relaxed. Turn off the television. Perhaps play some soft easy listening music in the background whilst you read these poems. Maybe even invite a few friends around to share the moment with you. Whilst you are reading why not eat some wonderful gypsy tart. The recipe is included in Section 2 of the book, written in poetic form by my good friend Inge Danaher and takes about twenty minutes to make with only 4 ingredients.

Drink a glass your favourite beverage won't you.
(Non-alcoholic I hope)

Table of Contents

Bright Hope

I shall love with the colours
Of a rainbow.
Wear white as a mantle
Of light.
I shall share invisible radiance
With sunbeams left and right.
Touch the hearts
Of the downcast.
Lift them from misery and woe.
Then, with bright hope,
Create within a glow.

Beautiful Happiness

When first I
Opened my eyes
I saw beautiful happiness,
Shining on me as a light.
It reached into my soul.
Warmed it with a glow.
I learned to love
As she loved me.
I shared my
Beautiful happiness
Til the world lit up
As bright as the sun.

Deep Thoughts

In the deepest thought
Come sweetest sentiments,
Longings to enrich the soul.
Yet in an unexpected surrender
Flows forth the rhyme sublime.
A thousand ways to express
Or to paint the canvas of life,
With words innocent in conception,
Until, when printed or spoken,
Become a feather to tickle,
Or extol the virtues and
Damnations of war.
Can lift a sorrowed heart
Or tear at the fabric of society.
Be careful what you write my friend.
Your words may draw blood!

Raindrops

If all the raindrops that fell
Were tears of angels that dwell
In heaven's highest clouded citadel,
What floods of sadness must fall.
Yet what celestial sun must shine
When angels' smiles come forth.
This earth no doubt shall be
A diadem set in a black velvet sea,
Majestically on her course,
Fulfilling her Godly destiny.

Let The Wind Pray For Me

Should I in all loneliness be found
Beneath the tree of wisdom,
Pondering thoughts deep and profound,
Ask the wind to pray for me.

Let no book withhold its pages
By lie or false acclamation
But speak to thee from all ages,
Whilst the wind speaks to me.

If I should lose myself
In cascades of leaves,
In treasures of man's wealth,
Let the wind pray for me.

To Scratch The Surface

From the written word
Are the patterns of thought.
Some mixed,
Some confused,
Some in complex simplicity.
Of all the things ever transferred,
By the pen of man,
Hope,
Wonder,
Love,
Humility,
Kindness,
All found in one word,
You!

Let Me Dry Thy Tears.

Your tears may flow like
Rivulets upon your cheek.
Wiped away by a
Cloth of unhappiness
But the sun will shine,
Drying those tears as
They hang upon the line,
With rays of sunlight
Given freely by
The God of Love.

Divine Moments

There are moments
Divine
Which kiss my heart.
In the loneliness
Of the night
Whilst separated
From the world,
Thinking of you
I am blessed,
Knowing you care.

"Between a pillow and a dream is a smile of love for thee."

Man Of Dreams

Where my heart lies,
Down by the ocean,
Stands the girl of my devotion.
Her hair aglow
With radiant sunbeams.
The setting sun all bathed in red.
Lapping waves caress her footsteps
As the stars rise above her head.

I walk with her arm in arm
Beneath the moonlight upon the sand.
With each step my love increases.
With each touch my loneliness ceases.
With each kiss my breath is taken.
For I am a man of dreams.

Where my heart lies
There are no tears.
In this moment of sweet surrender,
Beneath the skies of autumn splendour,
We walk on hand in hand.

She sits upon a majestic stone
Like a queen upon a throne.
The gentle wind her face embraces.
Then her eyes on me bestow,
A loving glance that's Oh ... so tender!
With each smile my heart grows fonder.
With each moment love is stronger.
With each word she answers yes.
For I am a man that's full of dreams.

Beyond Reaching

Stretched upon the expanse of space
Curtain cords and silken lace.
Filtered light from sun and moon,
This time moves by far too soon.
A veil of memory shutters out
Some distant life without a doubt.
Forgotten moments from days gone by.
I wonder why, I wonder why.
Is there hope in these short hours
To grow and grow like springtime
flowers,
To return to dust from whence we
came
Then renew our lives and be the same?
To drift and be a nothingness
Or wander through some wilderness?
I wonder if, I wonder if,
Beyond ... is there a greater gift?

Crematorium Resurrection Song

You pick yourself up
You dust yourself off
And you start all over again.

"From small wisps of wickedness may form great clouds of thunder."

I Shall Rise!

You may find me in the gutter
Down on my luck.
You may even find me
Feeling life sucks

But I shall rise!

My food may be all gone.
My clothes in tatters and torn
You may even find me
Looking down and forlorn

But I shall rise! I shall rise!

Though my family are taken from
My side, where they belong
And my heart wants not to sing
........Yet

I shall rise! I shall rise! I shall rise!

Though the grave shall claim me at the last

Hallelujah ....I shall rise! ....I shall rise!

"So what if your back aches and your mind feels tired. Remember it is for the Lord that you've been hired."

The Glass

Just as an empty glass
Can be seen through
So can empty men
For what men fill
Themselves
With
Shows
Others
What
They
Hold Most

The Child Above

The child above,
The child within,
The child without,
The child returned.
The heaven.
The earth.
The heavens again.
All tears wiped.
Nothing lost to God,
No not one!
All living matter
Accounted for.
All lost opportunity
Compensated.

Footfalls On The Emerald Isle

Oh Ireland, fair country,
A people so fine!
Full of character,
With hopes so divine.
Thy sons and daughters
With strength of heart
Shall arise with dignity,
This gospel impart.
There have been footfalls
On this Emerald Isle
For many a year.
With wandering smile,
They who were giants
Walked your land.
Leaving a treasure
So wonderfully grand.
Impart this gift
With each step you make
To the lands you are sent,
From night til daybreak.

Be Thou A Child Of Deity

Be thou a child of Deity.
Love thou beyond anger.
Grow into your potential.
Let ill feelings depart.

Never Let The Music End

Strings that play the heart.
Music that soothes the soul.
When you play me for my love
You complete and make me whole.
When you sing a song in truth
It's a pleasant melody,
That gently pulls the strings
Of the love you found in me.
Don't stop the strings from playing.
I hope you realise
They're pulling us together.
It comes as no surprise.
Never let the music end,
Never let the music end.
You've pulled me into love,
Let the music never end.

Lamp Post Love

I walked home a steady pace
When to my eyes a view I traced.
The dead decaying flowers
To a lamp post laced.

Then I, in pondered thought,
Saw kindness in those flowers bought.
A mother's grief in sentiment,
Love's heartbreak caught.

Beginning And End Of My Day

You are
The beginning and
End of my day.
My first thought
And my last.
My dream
During the night.
You possess my heart
Like no other could,
My sweet Valentine.

Valentine Soul

I have searched the rooms of your heart.
Found them warm and inviting.
I have seen the smiles unseen,
Touched the strings,
Played music that lies within.
Heard the song of spring.
Felt the sunshine of your soul.
I do not wish to leave,
For in leaving
I would not hear your heartbeat.
Know that we are together
In unison beating as one.

At The Edge Of Understanding

Where the nose is pressed
Hard against the window of heaven,
Hardly seeing what the future holds.
Only just realising
One must press forward in faith,
Hope, charity and love.
Accomplishing that which
The spirit was destined for,
Eternal blessings
Beyond the understanding of man.

In Heaven

I'm in heaven when I see your face,
The grandeur of your smile.
I'm in heaven when we walk a pace,
As I love you all the while.
I'm in heaven, there's no other place.
For home is with our Father.
We're in heaven …
This love has reached its height.
Hear all the angels praise
Before the altar of our king.
Let the host of heaven sing.
Heralds trumpet! As we bring …
Holiness unto the Lord.

Bubbles

There was awe and wonder
In her eyes
As she watched the bubbles fly.
Then reaching with an open hand
Chased them o'er the land.
Pop! Went one and pop! Pop!
Went some others.
Laughter filled the air.
Then she caught one all alone
That filled her with despair.
So gently to it spake,
Wishing bright summer days
Or sunlight by the lake.
Alas! Its life was short lived too.
What else could she do
But live with awe with all she met.
Hold onto life within her hands.
Then think it rather grand
To laugh with joy exultantly.

"Let not harsh words threaten thee but stand in hope of companionship with friends of eternity yet be friendly today til thy time comes."

Swan Love

How delightful those loving wings.
Your graceful glide o'er watery springs.
Thy slender neck in regal splendour.
Your eyes serene.
This my soul to thee surrenders,
Pure white,
Heart of gold,
Hint of charm.
For I behold ... Godly creature,
In all simplicity
Thou art a reflection upon the water
Of such great beauty.
Shed I a tear for no other.
This thou art
My love,
My treasure,
A gift
Beyond all pleasure.

Butterfly Morn

A butterfly came and rested
Next to my heart.
Danced and offered Nectar.
Shared a thimble full of friendship.
Then upon the wind she flew,
A memory held within a glance.
Watch as beauty passes by.

Papa's Lullaby

Baby,
Don't cry in your cradle.
Your Mama is coming
To cuddle you tight.

No Tears,
Shall dry on your cheeks dear.
Your Mama is coming,
To wipe them away.

Bright eyes,
Of clear understanding.
Your Mama is coming,
To teach you new things.

Hush now,
Don't worry or fret babe.
Your Mama will hold you,
Till your frowns go away.

Hold tight,
And feed on your milk child.
Your mama is here dear,
To nourish your life.

You are,
Most precious to us child.
Your Papa will love you,
Every day and each night.

When you,
Grow up and get married.
Another shall love you,
With all of their might.

Sleep now,
And dream of the future.
For we will show you,
Such wonderful sights.

Exquisiteness

The depth of my misery was
So great! So great!
All my anguish, heartache! Heartache!
When upon my pillow
The tears they fell,
They fell.
Then gave I away my burden.
I carried a new and lighter load.
A weight that was weightless.
I forgave.
Now my spirit is so great!
So great!
See
I hurt no more.
No more.
Do thou likewise and
Be blessed.

How Shall I Resurrect Thee?

How shall I resurrect thee?
By faith or chance?
By design or whim?
By knowledge unknown?
In the shadow, light,
Or before one and all?

By mystic incantations?
Dare I reveal power
Beyond your ability
To control?
Til the appointed time
All shall I reveal!
Thou art yet not
A God!

To Remember A Second

I look to the following day
Anticipating with reverence
One second upon another.
Yet I cannot live with recollection
One moment of that moment passing,
Whilst that second stands alone.
But as it moves into another
My mind's camera captures,
My imagination enhances,
My memory holds tight

But the playback button
Doesn't work too well.
So I think it worthwhile
To write and hope
That the paper doesn't get
Destroyed too.

When The Wind Blows

When the wind blows
Between sultry summer days,
Before winters icy breath.
When the children of the trees fall
Over brown and amber crawl.
While grey clouds of autumn
Rest their final watering,
There is splendour in the dying.
From crying new life calls.
Earth bathed in brilliant glow
Soon buried by the falling snow.
Vigour gives its last release
Preparing for a welcome peace.
Each season has its place ...
When the wind blows.

"Speak loudly with a soft voice."

Rule Thy Life

Let not life rule over thy love
Nay, rather let love rule thee.
For in all thy getting and thy gaining
What is life if there be nothing remaining?
If all thy fretting for what thou loseth
Comes from what thou chooseth.
Then nought but blame falls to thee.
So rise above unsaintly displeasures.
Thy wife and family are thy true treasures.
Let life take care of thy daily needs.
Thou take care of thine.

Dust In The Breeze

Bury me deep.
Deep as the grave
Can hold me,
So that all that's left of me
Is gone.
Gone with the breeze!
Catch me if you can
For I am dust.
Run across fields after me.
Run so the air brushes your hair.
Feel my touch
Hardly there.
Though dark clouds
May darken the skies,
The sun shall shine through

As a light barely seen.
Yet in the mist of your tears
I shall be there watching,
Loving you,
Till we meet again
On the distant shores.
Whole again.

Be Not Afraid

Be not afraid.
Though the last day of
Your life draws near,
Know that an ever-loving creator
Loves you so dear.
Perhaps you have not known Him.
Feel no need to meet.
Yet He loves you so sweet.
Maybe the life you've led
Wasn't what it should have been
But you are very important to Him.
Be not afraid.
It is but a moment,
Then He will greet you.
Be not concerned
Of your heavenward journey.
His gift for you shall be
No less than you deserve.
No greater than you can bear.
A reward is still
Waiting for you there.

The Journey

Step by step we go
From the altar
To the places of tomorrow.
Far away
Over hills and valleys
Beneath the skies.
Often in sunshine,
Sometimes in rain.
Creating smiles,
Wiping away tears.
Nurturing feelings
Within a home.
Raising hopes and dreams.
Summer then becomes autumn,
Where the embers of our days
Keep the winters warm.
Beyond the shadow of the grave,
There unity endures.
Together
Eternity is claimed!

Wishing Leaf

I held a three leaf
Clover in my hand.
Thought I,
Life will be soon rather grand.
It has to be ...
For luck will pass

My way ....
That day, I lost my job!
The next, I lost my wife!
After this, I lost
A fortune!
So much trouble
And strife!
The rest of what I had
Was stolen by a thief.
So much for the wishful wishing
On a little, green three leaf.

The Bow Breaks

We walked, talked,
Found conversation sweet.
Made moments meet.
Halted all time.
Spirits danced divine.
Today sipped nectar.
Parted in love.
Came twilight silence,
The stars above.
Moon shadows fall
O'er ocean waves.
She is gone!
I am alone
To search again.
Teary eyes weep
On ocean deep.

Grant Me Love

My love for you is so imperfect.
It feels as though the heat of the day
Shall cause it to wither away.
The only way I know to make it grow
Is to love you all the more.
If I say a word unkind
Through reckless and selfish thinking,
Water me with loving patience
Until I am refreshed.
If I argue with sinful pride,
Nourish me with simple kindness
So there's no room left
In my heart for madness.
If I fail to be tender or understanding,
Hold my hand
So that I may feel your warmth.
Above all, share with me
The sunlight of your smile.
For in all these things,
A man's spirit cannot help but grow
And in all eventuality
All tears of the heart
Shall be wiped away.
Showing in time and season,
A more perfect love.

"There is no timetable for happiness."

Petals of Nectar

They are like flowers in the field
With petals gossamer fine.
Painted as butterfly wings.
Lifted up to float upon the air.
On landing, touching the lives
Of spirit children with nectar.
Dissolving on impact.
Yet memories remain
Like seeds in fertile soil.
Buds will spring forth
In due season,
Nurtured along the way
Until ripe for harvest.
Coming from afar,
Teaching and learning,
Carrying to greater heights,
Never alone.
Recognized for who they are,
Servants of the Lord.

"May the perfume of the evening rose adorn your body and fragrance the footsteps you leave behind."

Longest Way Up, Shortest Way Down

On the very first day of service, in whatever branch of the armed forces one is called upon to serve, the first lesson given, is how to salute.

"This is how it's been done for years, you salute the officer's rank, not the person. A sign of respect. Longest way up, shortest way down."

At the graveside the officer salutes you. LONGEST WAY UP, SHORTEST WAY DOWN.

It occurred to me recently, that had all soldiers, airman, or navy crew, been able to live, and not had to sacrifice their lives, how much of the climb of human endeavour they each may have accomplished. Just living and experiencing life to the full. Climbing that stairway up life's mountainside of wonders. Such a long way up, learning valuable lessons. Loving someone, raising children and overcoming daily obstacles.

Then in death, by duty for one's country, in the cause of freedom, not least by the sacrifice of the family. One is laid low in the grave.

A SHORT WAY DOWN, but deep to the hearts of those who have lost you. This country gives thanks and salutes you for all lost opportunities in that perfect gesture.

LONGEST WAY UP, SHORTEST WAY DOWN.

I Remember Charlie

Charlie and me we heard of a war.
Somewhere .... everywhere and nowhere particular.
It did not matter......till someone told us why.
So we got in the car and travelled by and by.

We dropped off at the recruitment centre.
I remember it clear.
A little red board that said .... Please Enter.
Sign here ... You healthy lads, said the sergeant,
And here's the King's shilling.
I thought he had lost it .... he was so willing.
No! Not the King.... Charlie,
Fancy getting us into this thing!

The grub was good in the camp canteen,
But not as good as mum's pork pies.
Fish and chips and all the other delicious food I've seen.
It's another life, and right opened my eyes.
Luckily my boots fit me, they're size eight.
I thought they were great!
Poor old Charlie his uniform didn't.
He told the sergeant he won't wear it,
He won't! He won't! He definitely won't ...
Now he's doing guard duty every night this week.
I drew the curtains back in the barrack room,
Took a peek....
I think Charlie looks rather sleek,
By now he's had time to fix it.

ARMY
RECRUITMEN
OFFICE

Training was rather fun,
Climbing ropes and firing guns.
Marching around and enjoying the sun.
Charlie can't march very well.
Sergeant says … he's got two left feet.
Is it any wonder he knows where he's going!
Kept him marching for hours upon hours,
Quick March, About Turn, and...
Even frog marched if you please,
Right down to Jankers for another week's guard.
Oh! The army can be terribly hard.
Bull your boots til your face shines in them.
Make your beds til the penny bounces!

Exercise, exercise, lose those ounces!
Some corporals look like they'd give you a thrashing.
Poor old Charlie he'd been given spud bashing!

Before you go away to war you get embarkation leave.
We both went home to our house.
Charlie stopped off at the chemist.
He's not very bright. He thought the sergeant said
Get some embrocation cream.
Lads ... he was a sight.
He may be a daft bloke, but he's my mate.
If anything happened to him .... well that I'd hate.

Mum and dad they gave us a hug.
Sister Lily and Tom too.

Now you're home what will you do.
I think we'll go to the swimming baths.
Meet with the lads...maybe have a few laughs.

Perhaps try the cinema, there's Four Feathers showing,
Something special before we're going,
Kiss the girls or go dancing.
I'd love to see old Charlie prancing.

I know some lads that have got married.
Think they were daft. Too long they tarried.
But then again what can you do?
War fits an ill-fitting shoe.

Goodbye, goodbye family and friends,
Until we sometime meet again.
Blessings on you all in case I die.
Come-on Charlie before I cry.
Let's get going to the ship.
To Victory! To Victory, Hip, Hip, Hip.

The ship was huge and thousands waved.
Ironclad Sir Galahad.
Uniformed men all well behaved.
Bunting and shouting, singing and clinging.
Shiny brass bands and our ears were ringing.

The show was a wonderful sight.
Not for them that take fright.
Given for heroes,
Men of stout hearts
Men on ships that were about to depart.

To somewhere, everywhere and nowhere particular
To face the foe in their armoured vehicular.

The ship's cabins were cold and bleak
Bells were clanging.
So were Charlie's feet!
Sleep tonight ... a long drive tomorrow.
Then up to the front.
Hey! Charlie can I borrow
I've left my mug behind ... come-on mate.
He's snoring his head off,
It'll have to wait.

In the back of the lorry we trundled along.
Some of us even sang a song.
Not good for your ears, I dare to say.
But when I hear it, it takes me in a peculiar way.

Comradeship's a wonderful lot.
To rely on your fellow when in a tight spot.
Share in their joys and some of their sorrows.
To be by their sides when you wake on the morrow.
Tell a joke and watch them grin.
Heh! Sergeant when's the battle begin?

Timemarches for no man!
You'll see it soon enough.
War is war and war is rough.
I bet you think you're very tough!
There was no moon that night...
The trenches were wet and muddy.
Thick was the air with the smell of death.
And fear welled up inside me.
Put back that sandbag lad!

They're not to be used for a pillow
Shouted Sarge ... and
Collect up all those rats and put
Them on the heap.
I think we all wanted to weep
But none of us dared, not yet ... Not now!

The shells began to fly.
Bang! Bang! Bang! ... someone else has died.
Gas! Gas! Gas!
We fumbled for our masks.
Our stoic Sarge gave a glance.
A poor soldier coughs and splutters ....
Another wren has fallen.... has fallen off the branch.
Charlie! Don't climb up there.
Don't be a silly beggar.
Too late.......Too late,
A single shot rings out,
As loud, as loud could be.

Charlie! ....Charlie........ Oh no ...no.......
Don't be silent to me.
Wake up.....Wake up and be alive,
Open your eyes and see.

Charlie opened his eyes, light blue they were.
A face all covered in dirt.
His crumpled body hurt.
A gash across his forehead
Made by the fall upon the ground
Looked like..... Blood dripping from a thorny crown
His hands red from the gaping wound,
That poured out of his side.

They've got me ....They shot me through and through.

I think I'm dying Burt!
He slumped, and I thought that he was dead,
But he chose to utter these last words.
Freedoms worth fighting for.... and then he said,
It's getting dark...... I cannot see!

If you live dear friend... please....please remember me.

It's good to remember those who sacrificed their lives
Wouldn't you agree?

Fairy Living

She sowed flower seeds
Among the gladed woods.
Sprinkled colours of love
Till spring arrived.
There's sunshine in the pods!
Cast away the morning fog.
Hung garlands on the rainbow
That only she could see.
Collected dewdrops
To make a necklace.
Made conversation with a bee.
Powdered her face
With nectar dust.
Sat upon her mushroom.
Sang her gleeful song.
Placed a hat of bluebell shell
On hair of fairy fine.
Ate her fill of honey
Spread on a leafy vine.
Slept like a baby
Till night fell like a blind.
Looked up to the stars,
Exclaimed
My life is filled with wonder
As I fill life with mine!

The Night Of Sound

Tickle the strings
With gentle rhythm.
Strum and sing
To lyrical word dance.
Love songs
Deep with meaning
Fill the air
With sounds of memories.
Dance till the night grows old.
Feel the senses tingle
With anticipation of the good stuff.
Then live in the moment
Of the rapture of musical heartbeat.

Golden Moments Of Joy

Golden days of joy
Opened with a smile anew.
I watch thy face light up with glee.
My heart is wrapped
With the warmth of thee.
Gracious are
Thy ribbons and bows.
Your gift,
When arms surround in
Tenderness.

Penny Beneath My Pillow

There's a penny beneath my pillow,
Hidden from casual glances.
Like a treasure
I fondly hold within my grasp.
Held so as not to be lost …
Bringing dreams of you.
Memories of days
When first we met.

To this very moment where
We are held in each other's arms.
I would give my penny
For your thoughts.

Your imaginings are sweet.
Those feelings towards me
Tell me I am cherished.
A penny is not much
To offer for a thought.
Therefore I offer you my all,
For evermore.
With all my love.

Our Tears

Our tears are
Shed like raindrops.
Poured out in great anguish.
Filling these hearts

Till they feel like bursting.
As a dam that would overflow
We are drowned in sorrows.
Child ... where are you?
What reason
Took you from us?
Where have you gone?
When will you
Turn back again?
In time or eternity
You are ours!
Our love never fades.

Perfume Of Desire

The scent I adore above all,
Sweet essence of Love,
Is captured within my heart.
Held there by your touch,
Your kiss, your smile.
Worn with pride.
The Fragrance of you
Matures with the passing years.
Like a fine wine
Fills my head.
Takes away fears.
Brings joy to the very air I breathe.
Leaves me breathless with desire.
Comes in a lovely shaped body.
That is you … My Love.

The Gypsy Race

Upon the horseback,
Riding in the wind,
Along sandy beaches
As fast as the breeze
Would let me pass.
No Stirrups!
Knees tucked in
Tight against the sides.
His eyes wide open,
My eyes tight, tears
Streaming from the cold.
I shall win! I shall win!
I shall Win!
200 metres done,
Another 200 to go.
Passing the tents,
Passing the cars,
Passing the tramp,
Passing hoorars.
Hold Tight,
Don't fall off!
Keep going.
Faster boy faster,
Show me what you can do.
No Whip!
I'm too kind!
You have heart! You don't need it boy.
Come on we are nearly there.
Riding neck - a - neck.
I won't let you beat me!

I won't!
The line is passed!
Someone won!
Who?
We won! We won!
The race is done!

The Beautiful Vase

Fragile as a gossamer glass vase.
Transparently beautiful.
The roses in her life are ...
Made all the more wonderful
By her presence.
She holds precious waters of life
For all to drink.
She reflects the sunlight
In her laughter and smiles.
Made of precious love.
Placed in the center of the home
For all to see.
A gift from God for the family.

"You cannot stick one piece together.
Unity takes always two or more."

The Hope

You went suddenly,
Taken in innocence.
Hidden.
There are no tears
That compare
To a heart broken.
There is no wish
Strong enough
To carry you back
To me,
Though I keep the hope
Alive within.
Yet with the burning
Of each day
I have the memory
Of you.
Occasionally I smile,
Though the years
Have passed so slowly,
Waiting.
God willing
My treasure shall be
Returned.
In this life or the next.

When Love Comes Calling

When love comes knocking
Don't you hide and run away.
When love comes knocking
Go on out to play.

If your knees turn to jelly
When love comes to call,
Turn off the telly
Just let yourself fall.

Enjoy the moment you spend together,
Because memories are forever.
Time slips by far too soon.
Make the most of a lover's moon.

"When you walk through the valley of the shadow of death, let not the darkness overshadow you. Carry a lantern of light. If you have no lantern then, like the eagle, soar above the hill and mountain tops till the shadows lay beneath you and the sun casts its warmth all around, and the light fills your soul with joy."

Storms Of The Heart

Thunderous clouds can gather.
Lightning shoots across the sky.
Harsh words are just as striking.
I often wonder why,
Such anger we hold onto.
Resentment and despair.
If only we would let in
A bit of sunshine,
Perhaps a little care.
If you had the power
To hold onto a cloud,
And let it rain upon you.
How long before you cried out loud,

Being wet through can be miserable,
Especially when it lasts so long.
Let in a little sunshine.
Sing a better song.
Be as happy as you can,
Choose the better part.
Gently, blow away
Those storms of the heart.

"My tears shall follow me. I shall leave them in my footsteps thinking of you."

Oh Father Dearest

Oh Father Dearest
When wilt thou arrive?
Where will all the angels go
When they're descended from the
skies?
Thou art our light
From eternity to eternity.
When wilt Thou come
To the beautiful, Thy beautiful
Zion city.

Oh Father Dearest
Help us to be ready.
Full of love and harmony.
With hearts that are strong and steady.
Help us to face all our trials.
To testify of truth.
Live without hypocrisy.
May our lives be full of tenderness,
That wondrous purity.

Oh Father Dearest
Watch us as we grow,
So when we're fully ripened
We'll be bound in unity.
When Thou comest
To the beautiful, Thy beautiful
Zion city.

The Clock Of No Love

His loneliness is as lonely
As the ticking of a clock.
Like the rhythmic beating of the
Tock, Tock, Tock.
This half that is missing
Should be his
Rock, Rock, Rock.
The cradle of his love
That's steady and repeating,
Always hidden beneath a
Lock, Lock, Lock.
Who but the clockmaker
Can repair the sound!
But the clock itself needs be
Wound, Wound, Wound.

The Dance Of Spring Or Fairy's Song

Flaxen hair o'er smooth soft shoulders,
Eyes wide open to the summer skies.
Slender body of a ballerina,
Painted toes in your crimson shoes.
Dance the dance of the happy hearted.
The world's full of trust and love for you.

The clouds on high they're gently parted.
Your arms stretched out like a bird in flight.
Valley's below in all their splendour
Awoke to the day when you danced anew.

Ballerina, Oh Ballerina,
Dance the dance of the happy hearted
Throughout the spring until it's parted.
Come fill the heavens with your beauty.
Your rays are found in the drops of dew.
You are nature's ballerina.
You're new life after winter cruel.
You are the petals on a flower.
The pirouette of sun and moon.

Come dance the dance of the happy hearted.
Throughout the spring until it's parted.
Come share yourself with everyone.
For lovers love because of you.

The Small Ways

Darling, sweet darling.
I write to let you know,
To help you feel the love
That is within my heart.
Unexpressed in times past perhaps
To its proper and full extent.
A tender kiss or caress timely placed
Would maybe have wiped away
Such heartache in your eyes.
To enable the embers to catch alight,
Or to burn
With perfect brightness.
You are beyond a dream to my mind,
My wonderful reality.
Your presence breathes life to me.
Fills this soul with contentment.

Aye Aye Captain

The old sea dog stood on the barrel and pail.
His belly was large, his eye on the sail.
The captain's hat with bright yellow gold braid
Was on his head as he stood on parade.
A cry rings out from a sailor below,
There's a monster! There's a monster!
It's come up from the deep.
I'm being squeezed hard, I'll soon fall asleep.
How big is this monster?
Asked the captain with glee.

Fetch me a portion to have for my tea!
Aye aye captain, said sailors all.
Then went down below to even the score.
So frightful the sight that they beheld.
The great creature lashed out
More brave men were felled.
It's big! Said one, as big as a tree!
Oh no! Oh no! It's now after me!
The captain gave a disdainful look.
Who'll sail the ship if my sailors are took?
You boy! … Are you courageous enough?
Aye aye captain … You go and get stuffed!
So the big man with his cat-o-nine-tails
Went down to assist, show he was bold,
Or so it is told ...
For the only one left was the young cabin boy
To sail the ship, the ship Ahoy,
With a hold full of booze, the drunken swine!
Like the others ... had his fill
Of the rum and the wine.

"When the storms of life gather overhead and your heart is soaked through from the downpour, know that life's happiness will return to you if you learn to dance in the rain."

Battle Scar Living

Dying is a death not worth living.
Though it comes to all,
With impatience to some,
Reckless abandonment to others.
I shall hold onto the last minute,
Savour the last second of life.
Every illness will be fought
With hope, the battle won.
The scars counted for nought.
I will never give in!
Never! Never! Never!
Should pain drag me to hell,
Cause me to faint,
Make me cry out for mercy,
I will not quit the life given.
Till he who gave it takes it.
Then in the eternities
Recall every moment
With the greatest of pleasure.
The good, or bad.
For they will be me.
Sincerely, Braveheart.

I Love My DNA

I love my DNA.
It comes from

Mum and dad
And far away.
From centuries of
Forgotten names.
Now I play the
Searching game.
I grow a tree
On paper,
Or on my
Computer screen.
I share it
So it can be seen.
My tree is getting
Bigger and bigger.
Today I am not
Alone.
My tree has grown and grown.

Campfire Friends

Gathered to inspire,
Lift up and make well.
With words of friendship
Shared in confidence.
Hanging on to each other's words
As if a moment lost
Would be a treasure of time forgotten.
The fire of the camp keeping them
warm.
Greater still the cherished moments of
their care.

Who Am I

I am as old as the universe.
Younger than a seed unborn.
I own all that you see,
Yet you may be richer than I.
I am as poor as
The dust beneath your feet.
I can be trampled upon.
My wisdom is as a fool,
My foolishness a charm.
Though in my company
You can come to no harm.
If you were me
What would you see?
A leaf blown in the wind
Or solid mountain rock.
Water ripples on a lazy afternoon.
Snow on virgin ground.
I am many seasons,
Yet for many reasons
I remain unknown.

"The sheaves will be many some golden ones too and down will come blessings on me and on you."

Summer Solstice Day

Build a monument like Stonehenge
To calculate the time.
Then rub some fern seed in your eyes
To see the fairies fine.
Mother Earth her face is bowed
On summer solstice day.
With June comes the harvest life
To those who wend their way.
The hand fast rite is played once more,
Then couples share their joy.
Why do girls go chasing
After every handsome boy?
Summer madness,
Summer madness,
On a solstice day!
Turn your jacket inside out,
So luck will come what may.
Those who dare to look a fool
Will dance around the fire.
As for me, my dear friend,
The honeymoon's what I desire!

*"To renew our covenants over once more,
when we do that we'll open the door."*

Tender Hearted Country Girl

She's a tender hearted country singer
Travelling on the road
Sings for all the people
So many ways to go

She plays her string guitar
With a pleasant country smile
Her heart it wonders endlessly
Mile upon mile.

A new town
A new bar
A new song
An old car

She's a tender hearted country singer
Travelling on the road.
She sings a song in every town
True to her man at home
Living life on the highway
The kind that never roams

A new town
A new bar
A new song
An old car

She's a tender hearted country singer
Travelling on the road
When her days are over
She returns home to her man
She's a tender hearted country girl
And by his side she stands.

A new town
A new bar
A new song
An old car.

I Hear You Snoring

I hear you snoring
From the other room.
If I leave you there sleeping
You'll go on till noon.
I snore at night.
You in the morn.
The birds can't sleep either
From dusk until dawn.
There's happiness in sleeping
So unaquaintedly apart.
Cause I won't be frightened
By loud noises
From out of the dark!

The Blind Man Wants To Know

Does a blind man know when his eyes are closed,
Though he wears no special watch,
The passing of the passage?
Where does it take him,
Towards death and then what?
He cannot receive a message.
In the silence no ticking of the clock or
Candle flickering with tell-tale light.

Snuffed out and gone by the crime of time,
That came like a thief in the night.
No alarm to let him know what was coming.

Eternity.

For now the moment doth disappear.
His soul awakened, all is made clear.
Looking down upon the Earth, o'er his garden
For what it's worth.
He sees a pedestal ... a face without a smile,
And the shadow of a cloud gone by.

As eight bells toll, he has to go.
For there was no denial from the sunlit sundial
Of the hour it was that he passed.

He Carked It

The parrot stood on the burning deck
Squawking like a bird that's had a fit.
Ran about rattling his beak
Until he finally carked it.

He was considered such
A fine feathered friend
To all the crew of the ship.
Until he finally carked it.

Now there's no noise
That comes from him.
Silence is his call.
I think he's finally corked it!

"The flowers of the land smell as good in anyone's hand."

Child's Love First Learnt

Baby first experiences likes.
I like my milk and food,
I like my mother's smile,
Her arms around me.
I like the warmth,
Not the cold.
I like the sweet spoken word
But not the harsh shout.
I like my toys,
Not when they're taken away.
I like my cuddles and sleep.
I like to awake and start a new day.
I like to learn,
To see, think, to walk or laugh,
Not to fall or hurt myself.
I like to experience new things.
I like your touch and smell.
I like it when you tell me
You love me.
I feel good inside,
I like feeling good.
I shall do things for you too,
That should make you smile!
I think that I love you,
I think I do.

"To gloat is a mote bigger than the eye that demotes the insight of man."

Come Sit On My Branch

Do you hear my warbling song,
You, who at distance tree awaits?
Trill of musical notes to thrill,
Here at twilight,
Or morns rising dawn.
Does it draw you near
My song of malehood?
Will you arise from your branch?
Come sit with me and
Sup the daylights scenery.
In your eggs I shall delight.

Laxative Ladies

There once were two laxative ladies
Sitting on their thrones.
They reigned from morn til night.
Belly aching and not quite alone.
Both were waiting for a colonoscopy,
A coincidence it might seem.
Still fortune smiled upon them
For they each supplied plenty of cream.
Their husbands were laughing this time
But knew not the ladies had hatched,
That in two months from now,
Both would be likewise dispatched.

The Villain Nell

Oh! The selfishness of Nell
To the people she brought her a fight.
She is the villain of the vale.

Their money she took and left them pale.
She stole their loot by day and night.
Oh! The selfishness of Nell.

Her booty kept in pocket dell,
Held close to belt by pistol fright.
She is the villain of the vale.

Caught and sentenced to Van demons hell
This dreadful woman full of spite.
Oh! The selfishness of Nell.

Accursed leader within prison cell,
Smashed the Bulwarks lantern light.
She is the villain of The Vale.

Remember long this criminal.
Who sank a ship in harbor swell?
Oh! The selfishness of Nell,
She... is the villain of The Vale.

My Last Pair Of Shoes

We were friends that walked together
Through valley fields of heather.
In Sunshine or flooding rain,
Onwards in crippling pain.
They were resoled many times,
As I, after sundry crimes.
Trying hard to look good,
Like a pair of shoes should.
Supple without a pinch,
They fit around every inch.
Though people gave a sigh,
It was them that smelled, not I,
The shoes that is!

On my birthday they were free,
Within a box given me.
Altogether a stunning pair,
We walked from here to there.
When on my last day
We both made our way
To the box that carried me home.

Arriving and leaving
Is ever so revealing.
Thought makes reason stare
Of my foot treading pair.
For the coming and going,
Both times they were showing.

The Gypsy Wedding

Phandav le Gombo - Tie The Knot

Patshiv Abiav
Baksheesh, Sastimos
Devlesa araklam tume
Tooti ka va mira Phuri Dae
Mandi Rom Baro
Zhamutro and Bori
Mira Kralisi
Amen bata kerav glata
Mira Dicklo hi prey le dila
Salk y mandi ka var tro
Sutho My Ves'tacha
Te'sorthene
Latcho Drom

Wedding Celebration
Good Fortune Good Health
It is with God that I found you
Thou shalt be my wise woman
I the chieftain
Bride and Groom
My Queen
We may have children
My scarf is upon the floor
Accept and I shall be yours
Forever my beloved
My friend bonded by heart spirit
Good Journey

Sixteen Rocking Chairs

Sixteen rocking chairs
In circle bound,
Warmed by fire,
Both of word and heat.
Here the people seek
The flurry of ideas,
That sets thoughts
Racing with visions,
Wonderment and applause.
Your voices have meant much to me.
Quieted my restless spirit.
Helped me feel not alone.
Lifted me to a height
Of happiness
Whilst I was with you.

"Without Love
Sacrifices would not be made.
Without Sacrifices
Love would go unseen."

We Melted Into Love

From student days of years gone by
Their friendship melted into love.
Through study, song and dance,
American Square and Scottish Prance.
Then when the shores of Brittany called,
Such parting was sweet sorrow.
His first overture was met with thought,
Till once again he sought
On couch or bended knee, recalls
His quest for loves validity.
Then through the years of walking
Through valleys and mountain climbs,
Of the many languages they had learned,
Love was best of all.

He Was A Bolt Of Lightening

There was a bolt of Lightening
That travelled down the track.
Nobody could catch him
Not even the neighbour's cat.
The dogs were all short of breath,
The horses were as well.
Then as he crossed the finish line
Spectators shouted ...
Blimey Guv'nor !!!!

Santa's Cheerful Work

'Twas on a cold December night
When snow had fallen.
Beneath the stars with candlelight
Choristers all began their singing.
Flames their flickering shadows
bringing.
Glow on faces young and old,
Chestnuts eaten in paper bags.
Winter scenes of dancing skaters,
Christmas trees with baubles hanging.
Cheerful families all believing,
Santa's coming! Santa's coming!
Leave him biscuits one or two,
A glass to sup with joyful glee.
There goes he,
Flying higher, ever higher.
Faster, faster the busy being.
Now the silent night resounding,
Echoes chills of windy breezes.
On and on the sleigh it passes.
Over chimneys and craggy places,
Till all the gifts are given out.
His empty sack all crumpled flat.
Returns back home to Mrs Claus.
I think I'm done, I'm pleased with that!

"Seek not power but rather seek to be an able and willing fellow servant."

Scallywag Joe

Beneath the trees lay Scallywag Joe
With roots entwined from head to toe.
His spindly form all six foot long
With cracked pox face will soon be gone.
Not from decay or resurrection
But nightly jaunts of swag collections.
A meal each night before break of day
Of worms and beetles with mud and clay.
Onto his horse a ghostly grey
To gallop, to gallop then gallop away.
First he espies a lonesome squire,
Joe's eyes turned to red flames of fire.
He relieves him of course of his custom cuff lace,
Then frightens the poor fellow with a view of his face.
On through the night he rides like the wind
A toothy smile and a sinister grin.
Brass buckled boots from a sad hearted man,
He takes from whom what ere he can.
Not forgetting a shirt to put on,
He robs ye old store of one that's quite long.
A jacket with pagoda sleeves,
Is next on the list for Joe to thieve.
I shall be dressed well tonight I hope!
For the devil is coming and I want his coat!
Atop a hill on trusty steed,
A cry rings out for all to heed.
With tricorn hat all caked in blood,
He cries … I ride on to meet my love.

Worm Food

When I leave my body behind,
Here's food for thought.
Who gets the arm?
Who gets the leg?
Who gets the hairless head instead?

Will the worms argue for the best bits?
Glad I'm not a girl!
They may ask for the … toes
Painted I expect!

Fancy having to gnaw through wood
Just to eat your meal!
I tried it once
When the packet
Was tightly sealed!

Dust they say I'll turn to.
I'm not so sure of that.
Cause the restaurant
In insect heaven
Made a profit from my fat!

"He who pays for my grave buys my dignity in death."

I Shall Gather

Give me the mountains
And give me the sea
Give me the sky
And let me be free
    (chorus)
Over the mountains
Over the sea
Near and far
For eternity

I shall run with the wind
I shall float on the tide
I shall go on forever
O'er earth far and wide
I shall stretch out my arms
And gather my friends
From here and there
Till Earthly time ends

I shall gather my memories
Those days to recall
With those thoughts
I shall fly with you all

Over the mountains
Over the sea
Near and far
For eternity

Deep Tones And Long Notes

Driving down the evening road, playing old music just above loud. He awaits the next tune with anticipation because he knows he will do it, yes he will! He is all alone, nobody is there to grimace, though he wished someone was there to listen.

The moment had arrived. The same place just by the railway crossing where he always stopped. The people outside on the pavement waiting patiently to cross. Two and a half minutes the train will have passed and the music ended. Yes, but whilst it played Oh! how it played and he sang along to all the words, forgetting none because the music was there to help him remember.

The first notes long and soulful, full of meaning. His heart leapt. The singer belting it out like every word should be savoured and believed. He believed, his heart believed every syllable of the deep tones and the long notes. The lyrics haunting his eyes with tears.

He sang because he could, here in the tranquillity of his car. Every word full of promises.

The barrier lifted, the train continued its journey and so did he until the morrow. When he would sing again the same old love song,

Sunshine Eyes

You are a child of eternity,
With sunshine eyes,
That brings light to my world.
I see deep within your soul
An innocent happiness,
That fills my being with utmost joy.
I am lifted higher on wings of love
Because you are here beside me,
Trusting me for your care.
In this ever changing life
Of disillusion and hope,
I am always brought to peace
Within my heart because of your
Eyes of sunshine.

Mask

Your mask is made of bricks.
There are no eyes to be seen.
Filled in through time.
Yet from time to time you look
Over the top of the wall
Saying, I am here, hello.
Then popping back into your hiding
Only to be seen again
When you're ready to show your smile.

Lasting Memories

I am wandering through time
And I feel so inclined
To want to get to know you better.
Though generations pass
These memories will last
As I read through these cherished letters

You're my Mum you're my Gran
You're my Great Aunt Anne
You're all the women I have never known.

Images in my mind
Someone gentle and kind
Did one day perhaps you sit and wonder?
How they could touch my heart
Long after you depart
These words that still make me ponder?

You're my Mum you're my Gran
You're my Great Aunt Anne
You're all the women I have never known.

Were you courageous and brave
Did you fight away the grave
I want to get to know you better
Were you loved til the end
By a warm caring friend
Or taken to prison for debtors?

You're my Mum you're my Gran
You're my Great Aunt Anne
You're all the women I have never known.

These dear words that you write
Show a glimpse of one night
When alone in your room you were crying
Was he taken away
From you that very day?
What was it that caused his dying?

You're my Mum you're my Gran
You're my Great Aunt Anne
You're all the women I have never known.

Orchestra Of Life

If
Marriage Unites Souls in Concert
Becomes Expressive
Turns Hearts Entwined
Forever Onwards Oh Divine
Overtures of
Love

Play On.

Freedom, Order, Consent, Covenant

We need organisation.
Order maximises blessings
Of contentment and joy.
Do we need wealth?
If all wealth were equally shared
Where would be the striving?
If there be rich and poor
Someone would be discontented!
Unless the striving is understood
To be a blessing.
If each shared of the common good,
Each according to his ability,
To each according to his need,
Would there be enough and to spare?
Should compassion be left to fade?
The world of order might then descend
To chaos without end.
If selfishness lived,
The destroyer of all good,
The core of all that is wrong,
What then?
A moral code needs be the glue
That cements all elements of order.
Perhaps man alone is unable to
Create perfect order.
He might then by faith,
Implore God for
Wisdom and understanding,
Or die without ever knowing.

Can He order a government
Of happiness?
Can it be done without
Every individual's consent,
By a covenant to obey order?
For every blessing comes
By obedience to the principle
Upon which that blessing is predicated.

You Are A Friend

You are a friend
Beyond the measure of words,
Who makes all my heartache absurd.
You are a friend
Holding all my shared thoughts
As though they were treasures bought,
Then hidden in a chest of trust.
You are a friend
That has shed tears with me,
Years with me.
I with fondest friendship's love must
Thank you
For all memories created
Between each second of each day.
When in your company
Clouds open to sunnier views,
As it should between dawn and dusk.
You shall be
Forevermore a friend.

Now A Woman

She was preciously small.
Shyly hiding her intelligence,
An angel beguiling.
With love, innocent and pure.
With trust only a child has.
Contented in living.
Receiving joy from all sources.
Giving a smile that reached
Beyond the four walls of our home.
Then it came as disasters do, untimely
In the midst of celebration. Least expected.
Tears flowed in the bad news room
Whilst the torture of heartache
Cried out for relief.
Week in, week out.
Oh! Happy news where are you?
The hands of the clock revolved.
Her legs now gone!
They were alone in a hospital crematorium,
No memoriam! No service! No goodbye!
Her spirit remained in the remaining.

A song of love sung from the heart
Took away some of the pain.
From mother's lips poured a guiding lesson,
Conjured from an apple bruise.
Then in the awakening
Clouds of sadness departed.
Frightened but not alone.

Love lifted her up
To a height unknown.
She grew taller ... till
She rose above all that she was before.
After the storm, a clearing.
Now a woman great and noble resides
In the world.

© To my daughter, Stephanie Lush,
Dad.
March 2012

"Happiness grows every day with effort
A little sunshine, A little rain.
What is planted will reach for the sky,
Fulfilling its destiny."

Footnote: Answer to the poem "Who am I" is ... Inspiration.

Life Is Like A Book

Life is like a book, a hymn book. The front cover tells us what the book is about. HYMNS. Thus informing you of the contents of the book and what is expected.

Like the pre-existence we knew to some extent what to expect on earth.

Then there are the pages in the middle, a selection of words to sing. Sometimes we sing well, sometimes not so well. We can sing on our own or in a choir. It all sounds good when we sing with joy.

We have a conductor to keep us in rhythm, volume and unity. Likewise Heavenly Father sends us conductors to help us be united and to teach us how to experience joy.

Then there's the final cover, Death, after which when closed, we consider a judgement of our singing. Was it good?

The book may go up on the shelf but we can always take it down again to review and sing once more. So likewise we will live again, to sing yet another day.

How great and glorious will be the day when all families will meet again and we stand before God in praise.

SECTION 2 – Collaborated Poems.

Bliss

Campfire music, flames from the fire.
A starry night.
Familiar sights of wagons capturing the shadows.
A gentle breeze brushing my skin.
Charcoal smudges on fingertips,
As yet another log needs placing upon the cinders.
Together with friends savouring the silence.
Thoughts shared at random.
Your smile.
A sudden gleam in your eye.
Lifting spirits ... lingering memories.
The smell of fresh stew in the pot as it simmers.
A dog barks at the rabbit scampering through hedges.
Women are nestled in the arms of their men
Whilst twilight draws to a close.
We disperse,
Settling down for the night upon feathered beds.
Sounds of the forest bring slumber ... gently.
We sleep, we dream, we are happy.

Ronald D. Lush and Inge Danaher

Crystal Rainbow

Cold was the breeze
That filled the air
As Nanook of the North
Stood and stared
At the rainbow frozen.
Now chipping away
The fragments flew
Along the way.
Hitting the earth
Then melting as dew.
Collect he shall
Of the precious few.

Onward dogs
Carry me home!
This magical cargo,
The last of its kind,
Must arrive intact
To heal the mind.
It's crystal powers
Should weave their spell.
His ailing wife
Must get well.

The huskies race
Like never before.
Soon arrive
At the frozen shore.
He ties the team

To the hitching post.
He stands by
The open door.
She's lying there
Just like before.
The icy cargo
Now in his hand.
Brushing her brow
With the frozen band,
He waits expectantly,
Catching his breath.
Her eyelids flutter
Thus ending her rest.

Ronald D Lush, Lisette Kuiper-Tromp,
Inge Danaher.

Mountain Top Of Perfection

Mountain top of exquisite perfume
Wafting from valleys of lilies below.
Divinely scented fragrance.
Beauty of roses and orchids,
Creating perfection.
Your presence gives love
The greater pleasure,
Beneath skies of light
Or starry night.
Standing beside me
Forever.
God's gift,
A perfect treasure.

Ronald D. Lush and Inge Danaher

Farewell My Love

I never knew how much I loved you
Til you were gone
Til you were gone
I never knew how much you cared
It's all gone wrong
It's all gone wrong
We shared so much together
You and I
Days full and long
Days full and long
Through sunny and through stormy weather
We battled on
We battled on
I sit here all alone without you
With broken heart and shattered dreams
The memory of our times together
Keeps alive a love
That was so real
Farewell my love
You take away
A piece of me
That's gone today
But in my heart there'll always be
A corner just for you and me
I never knew how much I loved you
Til you were gone
Til you were gone

Ronald D. Lush and Inge Danaher

Natures Treasures

Magical lights, pink and translucent,
Traveling across the open skies.
Using the silence to wander around.
The fairy tree giving a tinkling sound.

Like Diamonds on emerald pillows,
Dewdrops cover the open leaves.
Nature's jewels a gift from God.
Admired by all who take the time.

Hold the view within the eye,
Forever kept inside the mind.
Pay attention wherever you go,
Wonders belong to those who are slow.

Ronald D Lush, Lisette Kuiper-Tromp,
Inge Danaher.

"Sometimes it takes ten plans to make one plan succeed."

The Wagon Song

The great push has started
We're on our way
The wagon is loaded
We will ride for the day
Our journey is long
But with faith in our hearts
We'll move right along
Yes we'll move right along

(Chorus)

So press on
Press on my son
Just ...one … more … turn
One more turn of the wheel my son
One more turn of the wheel

Sore trials may test us
God's spirit will guide
We'll stay to the course
We won't run or hide
When you feel all alone
Just pray with your heart
So God will stay with you
A pulling your cart

(Chorus)

There's snow on the ground
Your hands are both sore
From pushing along

Feel you can't push no more
Just remember to keep
The goal of your heart
There's food up ahead
Keep pushing your cart

(Chorus)

Our family moves onward
Each effort we make
Love one another
No never forsake.
Though grief may o'er take you
When a loved one has gone
Remember they're home
With the Saviour my son

(Chorus)
Ronald D. Lush and Inge Danaher

Rise Above It

If you often feel upset and others get inside your head,
If peace doesn't reign your life, makes your spirit feel like lead ... Rise above it!
If your neighbour speaks too loud and makes you frown ... Rise above it!
If they have a sickened mind, causing you to fault find ... Rise above it!
If their clothes don't look right, won't change that very night ... Rise above it!
If their language is rather crook, or you feel misunderstood ... Rise above it!
If you see all their mistakes, ask what would it take if the focus were on you?
Maybe that would do! ... Rise above it!
If they lie, cheat or steal ... Rise above it!
If they fail to talk to you because you're often in a stew ... Rise above it!
If your temper is too frail,
Put a space between you now,
Hold your tongue till you can ... Rise above it!
Every word misplaced
Will bring on you disgrace ... so ...
Rise above it!
The sharpest knives of all
Are the words we can't recall,
That destroy the very souls we want to save.
Rise above it!

Ronald D. Lush and Inge Danaher

Life's Salute

The curtain has fallen.
The veil ripped apart.
Here gathered are some
Who were close to your heart.

You managed to make
Your mark on us all.
Life's trials have passed,
You answered His call.

Those here present
Are feeling the pain.
You've reached the sunshine,
Are out of the rain!

We wish to salute you
As we pay our respect.
May loved ones now greet you,
May angels protect.

May the Saviour stand there
Without any disguise,
Enfold you in His arms
With care in His eyes.

Farewell dear brother,
You've made the grade.
We stand to attention
For your final parade.

Ronald D. Lush and Inge Danaher

Seasick Shipmate.

So, you're new!
You land lubbing lubber dog!
Lean over the side,
Then throw up in the fog.

I know the ships rolling.
It's hard to stand upright.
Put a rope around you
Then tie it up tight.

How was your dinner,
Did it fall off the plate?
You'll soon get your sea legs
To resist a gale eight!

Oh! Watch me feet now.
What the heck!
When you're done puking
Mop up the deck.

Ronald D Lush, Lisette Kuiper-Tromp
and Inge Danaher

My Swordsman

My Swordsman,
Part me from my chains.
Set me free.
Bring me liberty.
Let the sunlight of your smile
Create rainbows in my heart.

My Swordsman,
Lift me in your arms.
Carry me away
Across the desert.
Allow thy features to radiate,
Create rainbows in my heart.

My Swordsman,
Unlock my captivity.
Lead me to safety.
Liberate my soul.
May the glow of your countenance
Create rainbows in my heart.

My Swordsman,
Release me from my prison.
Take me home
To my oasis
Where your love shall
Create rainbows in my heart.

Ronald D. Lush and Inge Danaher

I Shall Serve

My Master came as one who serves.
Not with pomp, not with crown.
He washed their feet, healed their wounds,
Comforted all that were down.
He wept for all their unbelief.
Fed the crowds wisdom and bread.
Teaching more than empty words,
By example led.

His Father was His constant guide.
Love and sacrifice His fuel.
He often travelled by their side,
Never to coerce or rule.
He said, "Come follow if thou wilt."
He did not use the term: thou must!
Do as I do He gently urges,
Thus inviting us to trust.

Then He stretched His arms out wide,
Water flowing from His side.
Until His dying breath He gave,
Still He serves beyond the grave.
I humbly bow my head and pray
Give me courage every day.
Let me help my fellow man,
Like a servant where I can.

Father, teach me how to love.
Send Thy Grace from above.

Let not pride make me fall.
Let me care for one and all
With the mercy shown to me,
By Thy Son who set me free
With His ultimate sacrifice.
Make me worthy of the price.

Ronald D. Lush and Inge Danaher

Ancient Knobbly Knees

The Archaeologist digs up bones.
He searches far and wide,
Looking for a dinosaur
That's forgotten how to hide.
It once played a game of peekaboo
Many years ago I believe.
Its friend it gave up looking,
Was tired of being deceived.
When the ologist had found it,
His eyes lit up with glee.
All that was left of the Saurus
Was its tailbone and knobbly knees!
So if you play a game of hide and seek,
Be careful where you're concealed.
Don't leave it to future bone diggers
For your remains to be revealed.

Ronald D. Lush and Inge Danaher

At The End Of His Rope

Bring him before the bench
Came the command
Of the local magistrate.
A man of distinguished attire
And ready to demonstrate
The hand of fate on fellows mired.
These poor wretched creatures,
Whose lives are in their faces,
Creviced, windblown, dried and sore.
Bring him before the bench
Else I dispense
Justice in his absence.

Bedraggled and in chains
Brought they the man.
Resigned to his hopeless fate,
Miserable waif and penniless soul.
Unable to remonstrate,
His legs now shackled to the pole.
The wealthy onlookers
Sitting in the gallery,
Wigged, powdered, dainty and smug ...
Bedraggled and in chains,
Waiting in shock,
A prisoner in the dock.

"He who bends too low, eventually scrapes his nose on the pavement."

Bailiff cries here's the thief!
Said he of him,
Accusing without mercy.

Blood red coated sheriffs servant
Eager to accurse he.
Smiling with a grin so fervent,
Whilst lazy advocate,
Reclining nonchalantly,
Bored, arrogant, without shame ...
Bailiff cries, here's the thief!
Be done with him!
Lock him up in dungeon grim.

Order! Order! Order!
Decreed the judge,
With stern steely composure,
Ruffled sleeves and satin jacket,
Hoping for quick closure.
Scowling looks over Tom Tackitt,
Desperate criminal,
Scratching his lice ridden head,
Scared, beaten with little hope.
Order! Order! Order!
Repeated call!
Silence came upon the house.

Who accuses this man?
Blacksmith stands forth.
Man of muscular build,
Leather apron and sweat stained skin,
Respected by his guild.
Confident of an all-out win.
Admired by citizens.
Taking a very deep breath,
Throwing daggered looks at Tom.

Who accuses this man?
Aye your honour!
The Scotsman loudly proclaims

What evidence is there?
Shouts the defence.
A scraggly little mare,
Ungroomed, unshod, one eyed, limping,
It's hapless equine stare,
Looks to them a decrepit thing.
Pitied by one and all,
Now led to the center court
For the multitude to see.
What evidence is there?
This 'orse good sir
Such as is standing by me.

He stole my precious horse.
Galloped away,
Leaving a shoe behind.
A cry came from the dock - It ain't mine!
Why steal a horse half blind?
The kilted man's a lying swine!
Me feet are covered fine!
The spectators smirked and laughed.
Advocate fell off his chair.
He stole my precious horse,
My finest mare.
To the gallows with this man!

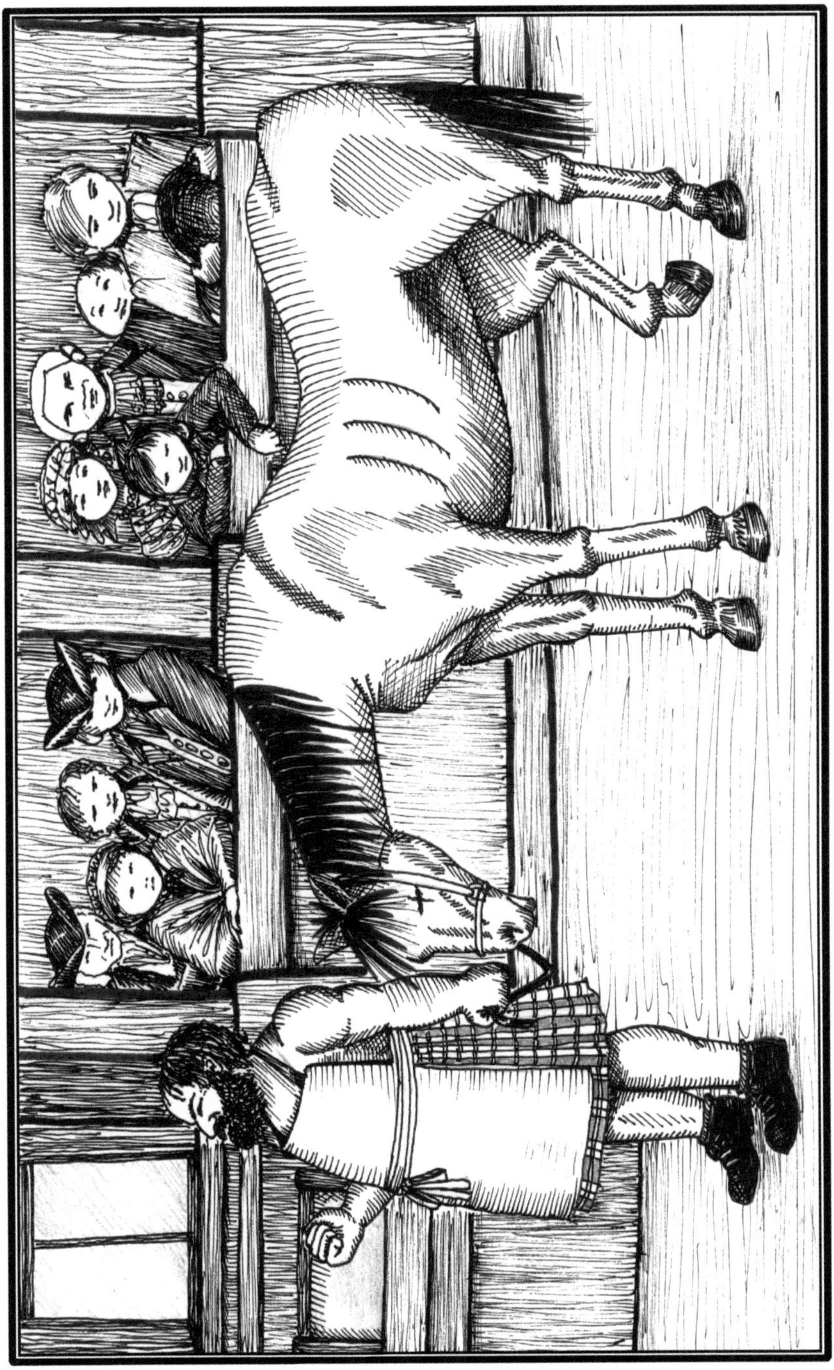

The judge declares,
If you speak out of turn!
The punishment is mine to give,
But first the truth we'll learn.
I borrowed the horse from the smiv
Said Tackitt with a beam.
Twas a damsel in distress,
Just like this she gave a scream ...
I'll have you in contempt
Noisy Fellow,
The judge put him in his place.

Let the damsel speak up,
The bailiff shouts.
Sadly she held her peace.
Too shy was she to testify,
She wished the trial cease.
Then brought a hanky to her eye,
Avoiding blacksmith's gaze.
All they heard were sobs and sighs.
Then poor Tom he felt dismayed.
Let the damsel speak up,
The cry rang out.
But never a word said she.

His fate was in her hands.
All seemed so doomed.
Ain't she the Blacksmith's girl?
A sole voice from the balcony,
Created quite a whirl.
Her face was now pure agony.

The judge he called, speak up!
Were you in the river dear?
Tom's heart pounded in his chest,
His fate was in her hands.
She would not yield,
Truth remaining unrevealed.

The judge he had no choice
But to condemn.
Wearing the sentence cap,
Declares you shall be hung tonight ....
A woman sighed, poor chap!
The crowd cries out: M' Lord, Taint Right!
Now advocate resigns,
Heads off to Wig and Cap Inn.
Bailiff grins from ear to ear.
The judge he had no choice.
Without witness,
The condemned shall surely die!

That night 'twas to be done.
They dragged him off,
The rope slung o'er the tree.
Mocking crowds came from far and wide
This spectacle to see.
The noose around his neck was tied.

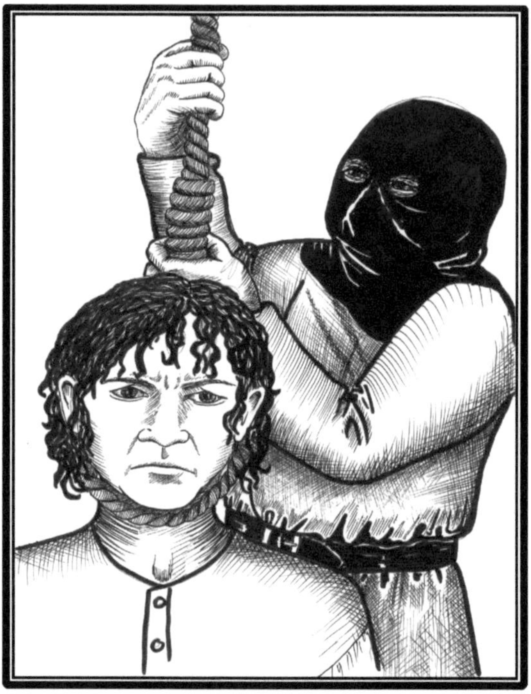

A preacher man arrived.
He blessed him as best he could.

Tom, he shed a hopeless tear.
That night 'twas to be done.
A Sudden Stir ...
From crowded streets came a voice.

Blacksmith called, Set him free!
Quiet went the crowd.
Tom his eyes seemed lighter,
Saw the father and his daughter,
His future looking brighter.
Tis now they avoid this slaughter.
Her testimony sure.
The girl finally spoke out,
He saved me from the water!
Blacksmith called, Set him free!
Give him the 'orse,
I owe naught less for her life.

Still standing by the rope,
Tom looks bemused.
Who will pay the hangman?
I've naught in my pockets, you see!
The Scotsman clearly can
Pay this most exorbitant fee!
Too right! He surely must!
Cried out someone from the crowd.
The matter was thus dealt with.
Still standing by the rope,
Tom spoke his mind.
I've something to say to you!

I want your finest mare!
Not one that's blind,
Ungroomed, unshod and lame!
Now is this all your daughter's worth?
'Twould be a crying shame!
Give her to me he laughed with mirth
I'll treasure her for sure.
Thou near took me bleeding life
I'll take your daughter for me wife.
I want your finest mare!
Take her he did.
Justice served ... Thus Ends This Tale.

Ronald D. Lush and Inge Danaher

"May every witness speak up for Truth."

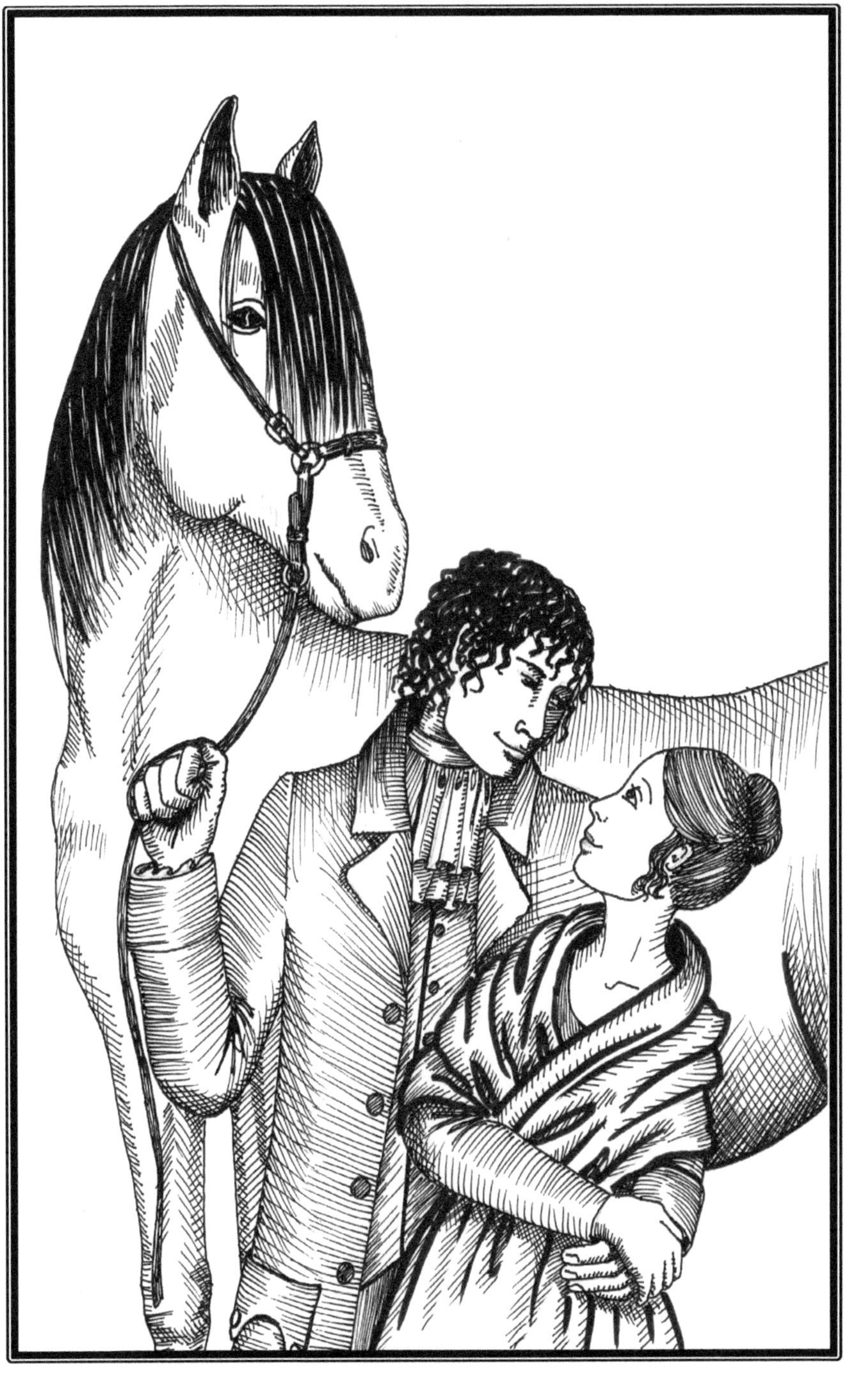

Chernobyl: Just Like Any Other Day

Just like any other day
Children were at school, at play.
Adults worked in homes, in fields,
Turning soils to hasten yields.

In the pool they trained, they swam.
Water flowed from creeks and dam.
Many shopping for their bread,
Planning for the days ahead.

Nature harnessed by their hands
Like in many other lands.
Fish aplenty in their streams.
Full of hope and many dreams.

Then one night whilst most in bed
The reactor blew its head.
Pack your bags they all were told,
Wear enough as it is cold.

Three days max then home you'll be.
Like an outing to the sea.
All were quick to flee the scene
But their homes … no more were seen.

I shudder and shake at the thought of food.
Desolation all around affects my mood.
The fish they swim in waters deep.
The Geiger counter makes its beep.

Debris is scattered far and wide.
Rusting through on every side.
Yet nature merrily goes its way
Nourished by the sun's clear ray.

Reclaiming land, the forest grows.
Blue the poisoned water glows.
Ghostly eerie is the place,
Deserted by the human race.

Will the world one day appear
Like the ghastly scene that's here,
Or have we learnt from this affair
That we must take greater care?
To be wary of our powers,
To protect the earth that is ours!
Ronald D. Lush and Inge Danaher

Christmas For The Gypsies

The day slumbered in the snow
Where early evening has its crawl.
Daylight's dimming lantern
Over grey white wall.
A steady Crunch, Crunch, Crunch
Beneath where footsteps fall.
Their families gather closely
Round the campfires beckoning call.
'Tis Christmas for the Gypsies,
They being so very poor.
For all their works and labours
Left them waking, aching, sore.

No food for the pot,
No food for the belly.
Here they rest for but awhile.
Then came the shout to move,
You're not wanted here,
Not wanted here at all!
We've done no wrong, they say.
Just tried to live our own peculiar way.
Still the voices shout,
You'll not stay here no more!

In silence do they move
Like shadows in the woods.
Gone far away …
Gone like the dying embers.
Stopping here and stopping there.
Rabbit stew today,
With taters and with cabbage,
Onions and some carrots.

Their fill was made more joyful
By the children's shouts of glee.
But in the night of Christmas Eve,
When fast asleep were they,
Some cruel cruel devil men
Whose hearts were filled with rage,
Set fire to a family's wagon.
They were trapped like in a cage!
Screaming, Oh! For mercy so!
Friends came running to their aid.
They beat the fiends back
Through the woods,
Then doused the hungry flames.
The weeping and wailing was Oh so bitter!

Shivering cold were they.
No clothes, no home to live in now.
The day was dismal grey.
A smell of smoke from burnt out hulk
Lingered in the air.
Frightened by what had happened,
All just stood and stared.
They dispatched a lad on horseback
To gather clans from far and near.
The call of help was trumpeted
For relatives that were dear.
The men came riding, riding,
To help them in their plight ...
Ready to stand guard
The remainder of the night.
Word soon spread to the villagers
Whose hearts filled with dismay.
Trudging to the campsite

On Christmas morn they say.
To offer of their substance,
Ashamed of village sons,
Whose heartless actions almost slayed
The poor and innocent ones.

They were met by angry faces,
Knives drawn in defence.
Laying food upon the ground,
Withdrawing a step or two,
The village leader spoke for all,
We offer help to you.
A brief and awesome silence
Descended on the place.
Then ... the morning sunlight broke
Like a welcome warm embrace.
A newborn baby's cry rings out
From a wagon in the woods.
A Christmas baby! A Christmas baby!
Twas enough to shout for joy.
Reminding everyone gathered there
Of another baby boy.
The peace of Christmas once again
Filled many hearts with grace.
Money soon was offered
For a brand new dwelling place.
Love reigned amongst the gypsies,
Rallying to each other's aid.
Evil being dispelled that day
As kindness was displayed.

Ronald D. Lush and Inge Danaher

Dead Alley Flea Market

Hipponimus Jones
Skulks in dark corners
Of Dead Alley Flee Market.

His wretched hand
All withered and worn.
The clothes on his back
All tattered and torn.
He laughs, He laughs
At the passers-by.
For he knows how to sell
With a wicked cry.

Come one, come all.
Look at my wares.
Just a sip of Elixir.
To take away your aching bones,
Lift your life from moans and groans.
Soften your skin like a newborn child.
When you lose weight
The crowds will go wild!
'Twas then one stepped forward,
A voluptuous dame.
Grabbed a bottle and staked her claim,
With a gulp and a swill
It all went down.

Minute by minute, she lost those pounds.
Soon all her flesh lay on the ground.
All her bones were gone, as said.
The thin lady was now quite dead.

People shouted, ranted and raved.
To jail to jail you wicked knave!
Hipponimus Jones had packed his gear,
Ran away with his bone melt beer.
The moral of this story,
As you may tell,
Beware what shady characters
Sell!

Ronald D. Lush and Inge Danaher

"Too many hours of bitter thinking brings about one heavy headache."

Eternally Yours

As you start your life together,
Having made eternal vows,
Always ask the Lord in prayer.
Don't be too proud to bow.

Ask Him daily for a blessing.
That the love which brought you here
Never wanes and never weakens,
And grows stronger every year.

REFRAIN:

Eternally yours
Is what you have pledged.
Not just for this life
Have you today wed.

Generations to come
Depend upon your love,
With those gone before
Rejoicing above.

Let the Iron rod now guide you,
Clasp it firmly in your hand.
Side by side you walk together,
Focus on the promised land.

Exaltation in His Kingdom
Can't be reached by one alone.
You must always help each other
Reach the footstool by His Throne.

REFRAIN

May the Lord reward you richly
With the treasures that endure.
May you often pray in temples
Making sure your hearts stay pure.

May your joy in one another
Be like on your wedding day.
May your home be full of laughter
Blessing all who come to stay.

Ronald D. Lush and Inge Danaher

I Want To Be A Film Star

Oh Dad! I want to be a film star.
They've advertised in the news,
They're looking for a pretty girl.
I've got such lovely shoes!

The audition is today Dad.
I'll go there straight away.
Wish me the best of luck Dad
As I hasten on my way.
...
Oh Dad! They want me to be a film star.
They've made it very clear.
Of all the girls who turned up
I caught their eye and ear.

When I got through the door Dad,
I was a little late.
My name was called out first Dad,
Some women glared with hate.

They all looked very glamorous,
Their makeup being fine,
With dresses so expensive,
Not as plain as mine.

The man looked me up and down Dad.
Had me turning round and round.
Then I had to lift me skirt Dad.
It was way up off the ground.

The director was most kind,
Said, I'd fit the very part.
The camera would just love me,
I'd be famous from the start.

I have to go to America Dad.
This could be my biggest chance.
They think I'm very beautiful Dad.
There's not much to enhance.

What part do I get to play?
I'll tell you this, and more.
There's a pilot in the air
Who dives to his death for sure.

Now I get to be a maid Dad,
Who's worried about the crash,
Screams and shouts and hollers Dad,
Then runs about a dash.

Is that all there is to it?
I feel you're not impressed.
It might be the first of many things,
If I travel to the west.

Oh please! Let me go Dad.
Let me venture on me own.
You don't have to worry Dad,
I will call you on the phone.

Well lass, says he, I'd like to please.
There's much that you don't know.
I never trust these casting types,
So I'm afraid that you can't go.

That was my one big chance!
For a while I was quite mad.
Dad's wisdom saved me from meself,
For this I am so glad.

Ronald D. Lush and Inge Danaher

Sunset Storms

Chandelier of raindrops
In the far horizon,
Where ocean kisses sky.
Crimson ball of splendour ... hissing.
Setting sun embraces water.
Sea salt sprays, expanse of sand.
Thunderclaps play their clashing symbols.
Cauldron bubbles atop the waves.
Rolling roars collide with beaches.
Foaming white horses run to shore,
Gentle swishing whispers on retreat.
Never ending scene of movement.
Stillness ...
Smiles the moon once more.

Ronald D Lush, Lisette Kuiper-Tromp,
Inge Danaher

The Broken Spring

I planted a thought within her head
Without a word ever said.
Before she knew it, she bought the thing.
Showed her friends the broken spring.
Now a broken spring may not seem
The kind of thing to make her beam.
You would not think very much of that
But somehow she managed to make a hat.
The hat got stuck upon her head.
Tangled herself in my bedstead.
She ranted and raved cause she couldn't get
loose.
Now she looks like an unfortunate moose!

Ronald D. Lush and Inge Danaher

"If you have enough spiritual wisdom in your personal bank account, you can bounce back from most situations."

Penniless Hopes

Christmas in a poverty house
Where none but the poor abide.
Nathan Fullahope sat quite alone,
His hunger trying to hide.
'Twas but a pauper's meal
Of porridge stale and cold.
A lot of starving mouths to feed,
Not many growing old.

Where in the corner of the room,
Biddy in her knitted shawl,
Staring eagerly 'neath the table,
Waits for all the crumbs to fall.
There on a metal plate,
A candle burning dim,
Is all the warming they get now.
This winter feeling grim.

Inside a tattered cardboard box
With worn out rags as cover,
Young baby Frederick starts to cry,
Then looks up at his mother.
A tear runs down her cheek.
No milk to feed her child.
Such heavens blessings in retreat.
No angels on them smiled.

It's time to sleep as twilight fades
Whilst twinkling stars guard the sky.
Though strangers quietly pass outside
Unaware of wants or why.

Cheerless wet is the night
As moonlight shines on pools.
Glimmering beams like wisps of hope
Are but the gold of fools.

Fullahope standing, looks outside.
His heart drawn by song of rain.
He follows some voice that calls him on
Through the doorway down the lane.
As if in dream wends his way
Over cobbles, now winding road.
People stare as he passes by …
Ever onwards Nathan strode.

Passing the baker kneading dough,
In the hours of early morn.
Now market folk rushing to and fro,
With all haste their stalls adorn.
By the bridge, close to stream,
Sat a child without shoes.
Starving, tearful, on its own.
There's nothing left to lose!

Onward he travels past a church.
Bows his head in sombre praise.
Led by the whispering in his mind,
These heavenly words he prays:
God I ain't much to see,
A better life I need.
My wife and kids they want some cheer,
From lack of hope be freed.

Ahead a mansion comes to view
With bow windows all decked out.
A table of plenty seen inside,
Prosperity all about.
Fireplace with embers,
Shadowy figures pass.
A woman's face now looks upon
The man of another class.

She sees him further down the way
Secluded from other's sight.
Good fortune smiles now upon this chap.
Three pennies he finds that night.
Pure joy transforms his face,
A vision to behold.
He thanks his Heavenly Father,
No longer feels the cold.

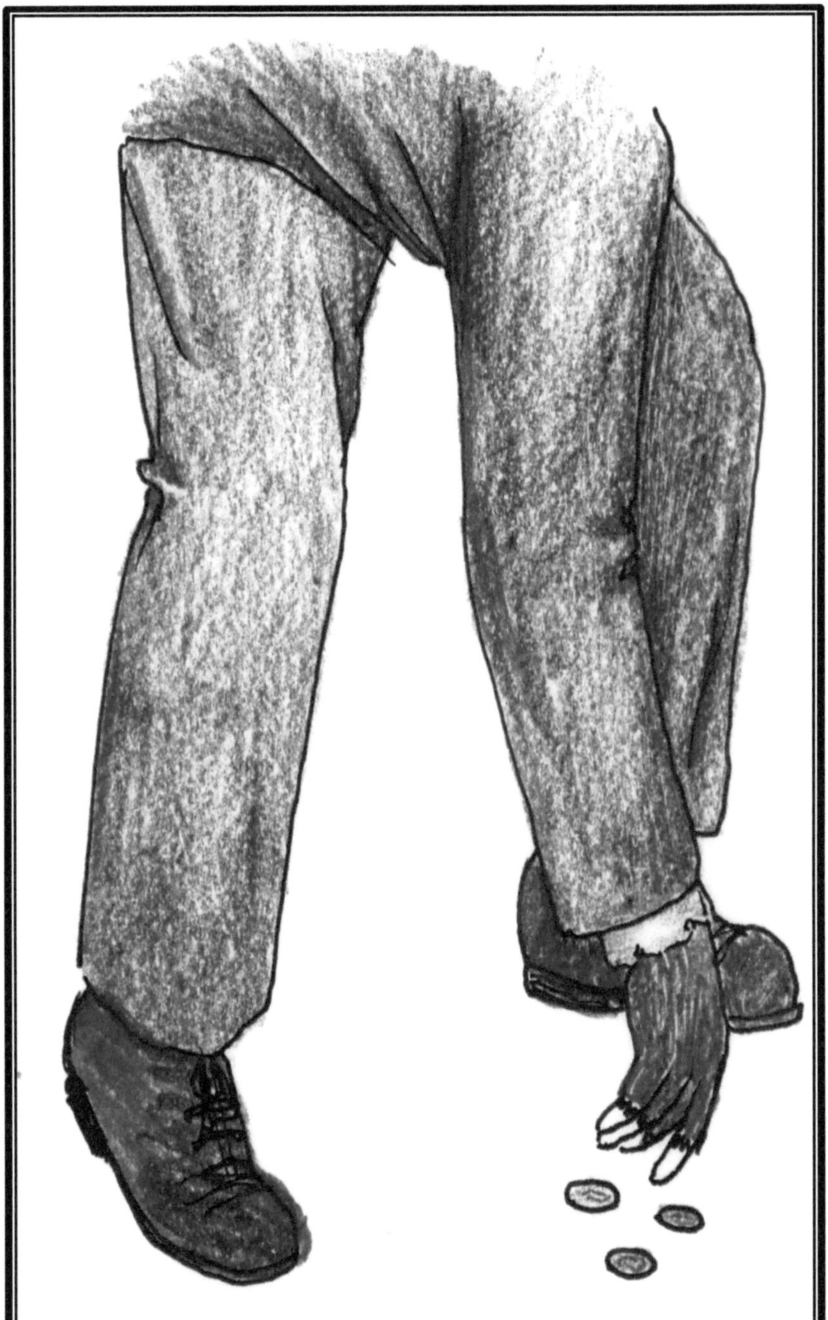

Returning on his journey home,
This Christmas carol singing:
"With wondering awe the wise men saw
The star in heaven springing".
Nathan skips to the beat,
Holding tight his treasure.
By river sees the weeping child.
Sadness beyond measure.

His heart is moved, now torn in two.
His children's eyes he pictures.
He hesitates then gives a penny,
Despite poverty's strictures.
Boldly resuming song:
"Angels sing Hosanna".
Retraces steps he walked along.
One child blessed with manna!

The market place soon looms ahead.
There sits a man dressed in rags.
He looks with pity upon this form,
All possessions kept in bags.
"Hosanna to His Name!"
A coin he gives with grace,
The heavenly star its rays afar
Shines down on Nathan's face.

Around the corner now he strolls,
One penny still remaining.
A blind man sitting in the gutter,
Wet droplets on him raining.
Holds out his twisted hand,
A sobbing message sends.
With heavy heart he gives his all,
His head he sadly bends.

"And with delight in peaceful night
They heard the angels singing.
The heavenly star its rays afar
On ev'ry land is bringing."
She'd watched him on his way,
Compassion stirred her now.
Stunned by such generosity
She made her solemn vow.

Back home his family gather.
The hunger not abated.
He hesitates, should he share his tale?
They eagerly awaited.

He tells them God is kind.
That somehow they will cope.
If I die without charity
I die without hope.

Was there not a gentle knocking?
Quickly they open the door.
A giant basket full of treasures
Stands alone there on the floor.
Heavenly angel's choir
Now sings in loud acclaim
The unending song of glory.
Hosanna to His Name!

When despite our needs, we give all,
When charity reins our hearts,
When the rich are filled with
compassion,
When each one willingly parts,
Then the King of Glory
Once more returns to earth.
Only then the Christmas story
Is given its rebirth.

Ronald D Lush, Inge Danaher
and Lisette Kuiper-Tromp.

The Unholy Porridge

Jimmy McNamara
A Scottish friend of mine,
He likes to tread the grapes,
He loves to drink the wine.
On this special day,
An occasion like no other,
He poured out porridge in a trough
Then made it for his mother.
He took his polished shoes off,
Then his tartan socks,
After jumping in head first,
He stood there in his jocks.

CHORUS:

Oh! Jimmy McNamara is such a funny bloke
But never eat his porridge for it will make you choke.

Now porridge without taste
Is a mixture without thought.
He adds a little this and that
And then some savory salt.
He stamps his feet about,
Dances a merry jig,
Then grabs the bottle of scotch
To have another swig.
The rest went in the brew,
Enhancing thus its flavor.
The tasty mess flew through the air
For the onlookers to savor.

CHORUS

The commotion that it caused
Made the women swoon and faint.
For a Scotsman without kilt
Was a funny sight and quaint.
His rather skinny mother
Now came into the room.
Shocked by her drunken son,
She grabbed the nearest broom.
He pacified her quickly
With an offer of some gruel.
She took a bowl and filled it
Then sat down on a stool.

CHORUS

The porridge seemed quite tasty.
She grabbed the biggest spoon.
Gulping it down quickly,
She swallowed far too soon.
Something caught her teeth.
It felt like they were chippings.
She spat onto the table
Some rather dirty clippings.
A knock came at the door,
It was the local priest.
His eyes were open wide
At this unholy feast.

CHORUS

He was offered a utensil
To make his fill for sure.
Then ate many a bowlfull
Before sliding to the floor.
Jethro Higgins came calling
From the constabulary.
Tasting some of the porridge,
Changed his vocabulary.
Now the moral of the story
Is be careful what you eat.
If Jimmy McNamara cooks
Make sure he's washed his feet.

Ronald D Lush, Inge and Dennis Danaher

Blood Suckers

Kirsty and Karen,
The vampirisim pair
Of nurses who work for
The National Health Care,
Started a clinic
For sucking your blood.
In the Queen Alexander,
Bout time of the flood.

In came a lady
Rather nervous with sweat.
They'd never a patient

As difficult yet.
No vein could be found,
Though they tapped once or twice.
She spat on the floor.
Now that weren't very nice!

There's a hole in the needle
Like a miniature tunnel.
They tried draining more
By an elaborate funnel.
Into the bag
Went the liquid so red,
Whilst Karen looked about
For an extra soft bed.

The tape and the scales,
The stetho and sphyg,
All have their place
In this blood-letting rig.
Pillows they took
Where they could be found.
This pair was resourceful,
So quick to confound.

They charge not a penny,
No squatters right fee.
One and all are welcome
In room number three.
Rubber gloves are put on,

Now emotions run high.
Some relatives faint,
Others moan and they sigh.

The clasp needs to open.
The blood needs to flow.
Sometimes it drains quickly,
Oft times it runs slow.
One patient got worried,
Had a tear in his eye.
More fluid was needed
Yet his veins had run dry.

Another occasion
Was rather absurd,
For all of a sudden
An accident occurred.
The dark red liquid
Squirted this, and that way.
Over walls, over ceiling,
Over floor went the spray!

Even though the end
Of this tale is quite gory,
To make you feel welcome
Is the aim of this story!
For at shouts of Oh Yeah!
We all join the cheer.
They slap on a plaster
And no-one needs fear.

Ronald D. Lush and Inge Danaher

The Gypsy Tart Recipe

First you warm the oven,
Raise from low to high.
Two hundred in Celsius,
It bakes a lovely pie.

You take four hundred grams
Of milk out of a tin.
Three forty grams Muscovado sugar,
Now whisk and mix it in.

Beat it for ten minutes
With all the force you can,
Until it's light and fluffy,
Has a coffee coloured tan.

Grab a ten inch shortcrust pie base,
Prebaked it has to be.
Pour in the beaten mixture.
Watch it cook with glee.

Ten minutes in the oven,
Enjoy its yummy scent.
Then let it cool completely,
A gift from heaven sent.

This tart is so delicious,
Fed many a gypsy man.
Serve it with plain yoghurt
Or crème fraiche if you can.

Inge Danaher.

Who Is The Jailer

Who is the jailer,
Who is the jailer,
Who is the jailer of the spirit prison.
Was it God our Father
When the universe unfurled.
To keep us out of paradise,
Angels guard the tree of life.
Do they also lock the prison
Until we've earned eternal life.

Who is the jailer,
Who is the jailer,
Who is the jailer of that spirit world.
Is it Christ our Saviour
Who holds in loving favour,
The keys of resurrection
Without conditions for behaviour.
Does He come to their aid
When the last farthings paid.

Who is the jailer,
Who is the jailer,
Who is the jailer of the spirit realm.
Is it Satan and his kind
Who mislead and make blind.
Methinks it is not he
Who will ever bend the knee.
For he has no power over death,
Nor can he give to man his breath.

Who is the jailer,
Who is the jailer,
Who is the jailer of that spirit place.
Is it the Prophets.
Those of latter days and yore,
Teaching them the gospel,
Till they recognise for sure,
Who it was that saved all
From sin and from the fall.

Who is the jailer,
Who is the jailer,
Who is the jailer of that spirit prison life.
Could it be those now living,
Who temples should attend
To release their kindred dead,
Their prison sentence end.
Could it be you and me,
Who hold the keys to set them free.

Am I the jailer,
Am I the jailer.
Am I the jailer of the spirit domain.
Tis time now to reclaim
All those ancestral prisoners.
Set them free!
Let them free!
Make them free,
By the power of celestial keys.

Ronald D. Lush and Inge Danaher

The Barberettes Of Havant.

This quartet of fine ladies,
With finger snapping clippers,
Know how to take care of children,
From the old right down to nippers.

They've trained hard and long
To get their N.V.Q.s
Qualified to the eyebrows,
Did time and paid their dues.

You can ask them for anything.
Boston to dyed hair fair,
French crop or square neck,
Perhaps a Mohawk debonair.

They will smile at you and listen
To any crazy story.
Counsel you with wisdom,
Then wash your hair to glory.

Others helped them in the shop,
With lightning speed they cut.
They bopped them everywhere
Til they looked just like a nut.

All sorts of people come to them,
They come from far and wide,
But when they get their blades out,
The people run and hide.

One guy talked non-stop.
Grumpy even sports a smile.
Mad Sarah worked with gusto,
Loving the blue-strip style.

The boss went asymmetric.
Ditzy favoured graduation,
Not the kind you get at school,
But the long and short creation.

They wash and scrub in basins.
Use scissors combs and goo.
They slap on mousse and serums,
Even do a perm or two.

One lady sat under the hood
To dry her curlered mop.
She fell asleep and snored a bit,
Then to the floor she flopped.

A man came into the shop
To buy the loosened hair.
That stopped the foxes digging holes
Upon his golf course fair.

Such varied characters abound,
Some with hair so scant.
Yet nothing is too far beyond
The Barberettes of Havant.

Ronald D. Lush and Inge Danaher

Barclay Bank Blues

I tried to get a loan
From my local Barclay bank.
I dressed up oh so fine,
Was looking rather swank.
Showed them all my wage slips
To prove that I could pay.
I don't know what else to do,
The manager said, no way.

Maybe I've got,
Do you think that I've got
The Barclay Bank Blues

I had a load of coins
Saved in my piggy jar
I counted them so carefully
Hoped my fortune would go far.
I carried them in a shopping sack
That dragged nearly to the floor,
Heaved them onto the counter
Which was opposite the door.

Do you think I've got,
Just maybe I have got
The Barclay Bank Blues

The teller took one look
At that mountain load of cash
Then said they needed sorting

Each in its separate stash.
She gave me loads of little bags
I stared at her in shock
I'd have to add them up once more
She pointed to the clock!

I think I've got,
I know for sure I've got
The Barclay Bank Blues

The people at the back of me
Began to murmur and complain
But I was so determined
Not to take them home again.
The silver and the copper
The pounds and the pence
It took about an hour
The atmosphere was tense.

I'm sure I've got,
I've definitely got
The Barclay Bank Blues

Finally I finished
Passed all of them across
The teller weighed each parcel
Then gave them to her boss.
Alas all that re-counting
Didn't really help at all
The manager still told me
No loan for me this fall!

I know I've got,
Without a doubt I've got
The Barclay Bank Blues

The tellers are so friendly
They try to make me smile
We've become the best of pals,
I've been coming here a while.
The bank pays zero interest
I think they rob me blind
But to transfer somewhere else
I'm not so well inclined.

I think we've got,
Altogether we've got
The Barclay Bank Blues

Ronald D. Lush and Inge Danaher

"*The End is Nigh.*"

A Lesson In Poetic Writing Using Nonsense Poems

Isn't it funny how people can write nonsense-poems and they can become well-loved over the years. This is because of the sound of the words. Even though the words have no meaning in themselves. Like for example The Jabberwocky.

How we read a poem aloud and the inflections in our voice, can determine the sound of a poem, soft and loving or harsh and angry, maybe even threatening.

Here is an example of one such poem. Imagine it is written in a foreign language and read it out loud. Giving whatever emotion you feel the words are saying to you. It could be a soft love poem or a threatening warrior poem.

Isme Doolu

Dey newali crondal
Poke Indu in the vondal
Ahhhh su su beondei Isme Doolu
Shay Shay

Crusto!Crusto!Lin De Vole
Uptoo In Tay Pole
Ahhh su su Beondei Isme me Doolu
I isme Vaylay

Inboo Iskay dadoo
Roo inpay woozoo
Ahhh su su Isme beondi doolu
May May shay

I read the above poem out loud to a friend, who then had a go at "translating" it into English. I did not tell her that this poem was written in a made-up language. By listening to the emotions and inflections in my voice, this is what she translated the poem to be:

My Love.

I send kisses
As the sun rises
Oh so so tender my love
Stay Stay

Awake! Awake! In the dawn
Sun sends its rays
Oh so so my precious love
Be my joy

You give meaning
To the day
Oh so so my forever love
please please stay

Have a go at writing your own nonsense-poem or use the one below and read it out loud using either the voice of a child, woman or man. Read it softly then read it harshly.

WHALA!

Whala! Whala! Whala!
Myumbi imbucala
Day isi Dondi hey
Ondu Hubi isti bey.

Poetry is not just about giving a message. It is about the beauty in the sound of language. Keep that in mind when writing your poems. Let them speak with rhythm and let the words paint a picture just by their sounds. Although in this book there are pictures that have been created solely because of my joy for a friend's artwork.

Recommended Reading

Book of psalms
Shakespeare sonnets
Morning express by Sassoon
The cloud by Shelly
She walks in beauty by Lord Byron
Albert and the lion by Marriott Edgar
Works of Goethe
Gus the theatre cat by T.S. Eliot
Song of Hiawatha by Longfellow
The Pied Piper Of Hamlin by Robert Browning
Touched by an angel by Maya Angelou
The man from Snowy River by Banjo Patterson
How do I love thee by Elizabeth Barrett Browning
Poems by Edgar Allan Poe
The Charge of the Light Brigade by Alfred, Lord Tennyson
In Flanders Fields by John McCrae
I wandered lonely as a cloud by William Wordsworth
Lady of Shalott by Alfred Lord Tennyson
Highwayman by Alfred Noyes
The wreck on highway 109 Ruth Gillis
Poetic works of Pam Ayres
Desiderata poem by Max Ehrmann 1927

Types of Poetic Styles

There are many types of Poetic Style or Form used in Poetry. The following list is a sampling. Refer to the internet for more details on each form or for a more comprehensive list.

FORM	DESCRIPTION
ABC	Five lines which create a mood or feeling. First word of lines 1 to 4 is in alphabetical order, line 5 can start with any letter. Anger rises quickly Be slow to speak your mind Careful what you say Don't ever be unkind Once uttered words can't be recalled.
Acrostic	First letter of each verse will create a word or message: **L**earning to give **O**f yourself **V**aluing another **E**nduring trials.
Ballad	Tells a story like a legend and may also use a repeated refrain. An example of a Ballad could my poem "I Remember Charlie"
Ballade	Three verses of seven, eight or ten lines and a shorter final verse of four or five lines.

FORM	DESCRIPTION
Blank Verse	Form of Poetry resembling rhythms of speech created by using short syllables. Something like my poem "The Child Above"
Bio	A biographical poem. As an example see the poem in this book called "I Want to be a Film Star" which is an anecdote out of my mother's life.
Burlesque	Treats serious subjects in a funny/humorous way. See my poem "Worm Food"
Carpe Diem	Poems with a theme of living for today. There are quite a number of poems in this book that fit into this form. Such as "To Remember a Second", "Be not Afraid", "Rule thy Life".
Cinquain	Five lines where Line 1 has one word (title) line 2 has 2 words that describe the title. Line 3 has three words that tell the action. Line 4 has four words that express feeling and line 5 has one word which recalls the title. Flower Sweet, Fragrant, Inviting, Enchanting, Pleasing Evoking feelings of joy Lilac

FORM	DESCRIPTION
Chiasma	Chiasmic poetry is a Hebrew form of poetry which does not rhyme but uses parallelism to emphasise or explain an idea. For an in-depth explanation refer to http://www.journal33.org/bible/html/hebpoet.htm
Collaborative	Where 2 or more people collaborate to write a poem. Poems in Section 2 are all examples
Concrete	This is also called "Size Poetry" Writing the poem in a certain shape to denote the object. See my poem "The Glass"
Couplet	Rhyming stanzas of 2 lines each. The poem "Chernobyl: Just like any other day" is an example of a Couplet
Epic	Long serious poem relating a story about a person such as "Penniless Hopes" in this book.
Epigram	Short ironic poem derived from the Greek word "epigramma" meaning inscription
Epitaph	A poem written for the deceased and usually appears on a tombstone
Free Verse	Can be rhymed or unrhymed poetry with no set metrical pattern

FORM	DESCRIPTION
Haiku	Japanese style of poetry which is usually 3 or 5 lines of set syllables. Following is an example written by Inge Danaher: Water so common, Oceans deep, fathomless, wide People die thirsting.
Humorous	Funny Poems. See "The Barbaretts of Havant" and "Barclay Bank Blues"
Iambic Pentameter	Five sets of short and long sounding syllables.
Idyll	Describing either a peaceful scene or talking about a bygone era or hero. See "Mountain Top of Perfection".
Lay	Long Narrative poem often sung, an example here could be "The Unholy Porridge"
Limerick	Humorous Poem with a set pattern.
List	List of terms or events in a poem
Name	Using the first letter of each line the poem describes the word created
Ode	Meditative long rhythmic poem
Prose	Written in prose instead of verse but preserving poetic imagery. An example in this book is my poem "Deep Tones and Long Notes"
Rant	Free verse prose poetry written about a vexing subject.

FORM	DESCRIPTION
Rhyme	A poem written where there is a pattern of rhyming in the last word. Quite a few Rhyming Poems in this book
Shape	A type of concrete poem where the poem is written in the shape of the object. See "The Glass"
Songs	Some people consider songs as poetry set to music.
Sonnet	Usually 14 lines using a rather conventional rhyming scheme.
Tanka	Japanese Poetry. Each poem has 5 lines with set number of syllables. Following is a Tanka written by Inge Danaher: The Proposal. He proposed to her Whilst she was driving the car Her heart raced with fear Smiling he asked for first kiss Then came thirty years of bliss
Tercet	Three lines of Poetry either as 3 lines per verse or 3 lines per poem. For instance see "Crematorium Resurrection Song"
Three Word Poem Form	Tells a story with 3 words per line. My Poem "The Bow Breaks" is a Three Word Poem.
Villanelle	Nineteen line poem in a very specific type of rhyme. An example in this book is the poem: "The Villain Nell

Other Books

Original Publications (2012):

- Bright Hope original paperback version (limited distribution)
- Bright Hope leather-bound (limited edition - 2 copies only published)

eBooks (published 2015)

- Bright Hope
- *Grant Me Love
- *Let The Wind Pray for Me
- *Vision With a View

(* Note: the above 3 eBooks are also published as one paperback book called "Fishing for a Poem)

Paperbacks (published 2015):

- Bright Hope revised (black and white illustrations)
- Bright Hope revised (full colour illustrations)
- Fishing for a Poem (*also published separately as 3 eBooks)

www.ingramcontent.com/pod-product-compliance
Lightning Source LLC
Chambersburg PA
CBHW041612220426
43669CB00001B/7
* 9 7 8 0 9 8 0 8 6 4 6 9 4 *